...IF YOU GREW UP WITH
·ABRAHAM LINCOLN·

by Ann McGovern
illustrated by Brinton Turkle

SCHOLASTIC INC.
New York Toronto London Auckland Sydney Tokyo

No part of this publication may be reproduced in whole or in part, or stored in a retrieval system, or transmitted in any form or by any means, electronic, mechanical, photocopying, recording, or otherwise, without written permission of the publisher. For information regarding permission, write to Scholastic Inc., 730 Broadway, New York, NY 10003.

ISBN 0-590-33631-2

Reading level is determined by using the Spache Readability Formula. 3.2 signifies high 3rd grade level.

Text copyright © 1966 by Ann McGovern. Illustrations © 1966 by Brinton Turkle. All rights reserved. This edition is published by Scholastic Inc.

12 11 10 9 8 7 6 5 4 3 2 1   2   5 6 7 8 9/8 0/9

You may also want to read these books by Ann McGovern*

If You Lived in Colonial Times
Christopher Columbus
Wanted Dead or Alive: The Story of Harriet Tubman

*Available from Scholastic Inc.

CONTENTS

*A*braham Lincoln grew up on the frontier of Kentucky and Indiana. Life would have been very different for a boy growing up in the East or in the South.

In this book I want to give you an idea of what it was like to grow up with Lincoln and to live in the same places that he lived:

— as a boy in Kentucky and Indiana

— as a young man in the prairie town of New Salem, Illinois

— later in the city of Springfield, Illinois.

Lincoln lived in Springfield for twenty-four years. He left Springfield in 1861 when he went to Washington, D.C., as President of the United States.

Where would you live?

If you grew up with Abraham Lincoln, you would live on the frontier.

Abe Lincoln was born in 1809 in Kentucky. The woods were full of birds and wild animals. But there were not many people.

When Abe was born, his ten-year-old cousin, Dennis Hanks, had to walk two miles to the Lincoln cabin to see him.

When Abe was two years old, the Lincoln family moved ten miles away to Knob Creek Farm. Now Abe and his sister, Sarah, had a chance to see more people. They lived closer to other settlers.

Most of the people in the United States lived in the eastern part of the country. As the East began to get more crowded, more and more people moved West.

When Abe was almost eight, the family moved again. This time they moved from Kentucky to the new state of Indiana. Now there were nineteen states in the United States.

It took the Lincoln family many days to get to Indiana. They had to travel a hundred miles on horseback. They loaded the two horses with the pots and pans and bedding they would need.

Sometimes they rode. Sometimes they walked. They crossed the Ohio River by ferry.

They had to travel through dark woods. Many times, Abe's father had to get off his horse. He had to chop away bushes and vines to make a path in the woods so they could get through. And at last they reached the land that would be their home for fourteen years.

In Indiana, Abe Lincoln grew to be a man.

What kind of house would you live in?

You would live in a cabin.

Most cabins on the frontier had only one room.

If your cabin was like the Lincoln cabin in Indiana, it would not have a window or a real door. The door would be an open place in the side of the cabin, covered by a bearskin. And the cabin would have a dirt floor.

The cabin would be made of logs. Spaces between the logs were filled in with clay or with moss or mud.

A fire burned in the big fireplace. The fire

was used for cooking and for keeping the cabin warm in the winter. The fireplace gave light, too. When the Lincolns wanted brighter light, they could burn pine knots.

Abe's mother, father, and sister slept near the fireplace. But Abe didn't sleep there.

He slept in a loft under the roof. There was no stairway to the loft — just a row of wooden pegs in the wall. At night, Abe climbed the ladder of pegs to the loft. The roof of the loft was so low that he had to be careful not to bump his head.

Abe slept on a pile of cornhusks on the floor. A bearskin was his blanket.

Sometimes rain and snow came through cracks in the roof. Some winter mornings when Abe woke up he found his bearskin blanket covered with snow.

This was the cabin the Lincoln family lived in when Abe's mother got sick and died.

The next year Abe's father got married again. The new Mrs. Lincoln made Mr. Lincoln fix up the cabin. He patched the roof to keep out snow and rain. He made a wooden floor, a real door on leather hinges, and a window. He did not have glass, so he covered the window with oiled paper to let in some light.

What was the furniture like?

Most cabins had plain furniture. Most of the furniture on the frontier was made at home. Poles were stuck in the wall at one end and held up by posts at the other end. This made the frame for the bed. The mattress was usually made of cornhusks. Tables and stools were made out of slabs of wood.

Abe's father, Tom Lincoln, was a carpenter, but he didn't spend a lot of time making furniture for his own cabin.

If your family wanted a cupboard or a chair, Abe Lincoln's father might make it.

Some people brought fine furniture with them when they came to live on the frontier.

Abe and his sister Sarah never had any fine furniture in their cabin until their stepmother came to Indiana. The new Mrs. Lincoln brought feather mattresses and pillows and quilts for the beds. She brought a table and a set of chairs and a beautiful black walnut chest of drawers with her. Mrs. Lincoln said the chest cost forty-five dollars.

Mrs. Lincoln climbed the ladder to the loft. She took a feather mattress up with her. Then she took the cornhusks Abe had been sleeping on and put them outside. She said they would be good for a pigpen.

What kind of clothes did people wear on the frontier?

People on the frontier did not wear fancy clothes. All the clothes were made at home.

Men hunted deer and used the deerskins to make pants and jackets and shoes. They called the deerskin *buckskin*.

Women knitted woolen socks for the whole family. They made linen yarn and wool yarn on their spinning wheels. Then they wove the yarns into a rough cloth called linsey-woolsey.

In winter, Abe and the other boys on the frontier wore linsey-woolsey shirts, buckskin pants called breeches, buckskin jackets, and buckskin moccasins. A coonskin cap with a tail hanging down in back kept a boy's head warm.

Buckskin breeches were fine — unless you got caught in the rain. Then the breeches would shrink. As they dried, the breeches would get tighter and tighter around your legs. Abe had a blue mark on each leg all his life, from wearing buckskin breeches that shrank after a rain.

In summer, boys wore breeches made of linsey-woolsey.

Girls wore long linsey-woolsey dresses. They wore sunbonnets in the summer and capes with hoods in the winter.

In summer, everyone went barefoot most of the time. People carried their shoes to church. They put them on to go inside.

When Abe was seventeen, he took a job cutting wood. Instead of money, he asked for enough white cloth for a fine shirt.

Another time he worked for cloth for a pair of pants. He cut logs and split them into rails for fences. He had to split about a thousand rails before he had enough cloth for the pants.

Where did people get their food?

Boys and girls gathered nuts and berries and wild fruit in the woods.

Men and boys went hunting in the woods for rabbits, squirrels, bear, deer, wild ducks, and turkeys.

They went fishing in the rivers and streams for catfish, perch, and bass.

Most families kept pigs so they could have sausages, ham, and bacon. They kept a cow for milk, butter, and cheese.

People grew their own vegetables. Tom Lincoln planted potatoes, turnips, cabbage, beets, pumpkin, squash, and corn.

Corn was ground into corn meal at the mill. The corn meal was made into corn bread.

As soon as a boy was old enough to ride a horse, his job was to take the corn to the mill to be ground. The mill was a good place to meet with other boys.

If you lived on the frontier, you wouldn't have to buy much food at the store. Maybe you would buy flour, salt, coffee, and tea. Sugar cost too much for most people. Sometimes they would buy molasses to sweeten their food. Sometimes they got honey from bee-hives they found in the woods.

Once in a while, especially in the winter, you might have nothing but potatoes for supper. That happened to the Lincoln family.

Always, before every meal, Tom Lincoln said a blessing for the food.

"We thank thee, Lord, for these blessings," he said.

Abe looked at the potatoes. "Mighty poor blessings," he joked.

Would you work hard on the frontier?

There was no end to the work that had to be done.

Girls helped their mothers wash, cook, and sew buckskin into shirts and pants. They helped spin, weave, and make soap. Even a five-year-old boy was big enough to help with the planting. He could drop pumpkin seeds between the hills of corn.

Abe did.

By the time Abe was seven, his father gave him an axe. Abe kept the woodbox filled with logs for the fire.

He cleaned out the ashes from the fireplace.

He picked berries, nuts, and grapes in the woods.

When the Lincoln family moved to Indiana, there was more work to be done. Abe helped his father build the new log cabin.

There was no running water in a log cabin. Whenever the well went dry, Abe had to walk a mile to the nearest spring and had to carry water home.

He helped his father farm. He plowed. He planted. He weeded.

He chopped down trees. He split logs into rails for fences.

People on the frontier said that a rail fence should be horse-high, bull-strong, and pig-tight. That meant it should be high enough so a horse could not jump over it. It should be strong enough so a bull could not push it over. And it should be tight enough so a pig could not squeeze through it.

Abe made many rail fences that were horse-high, bull-strong, and pig-tight.

If a man didn't need his son to help him on the farm, he sent him to work for neighbors.

What would you do with the money you earned?

The money you earned, you were supposed to give to your father. That was the law.

When a boy became twenty-one years old, he could keep the money he earned.

Boys on the frontier did not get paid much for their work. Abe was hired out to farmers for twenty-five cents a day.

When he was sixteen, Abe went to work for James Taylor. He helped with the farmwork and the housework, and ran a ferry on the Ohio River.

One day two men asked Abe to row them to a steamboat in the middle of the river.

When the men were on board the steamboat, each of them threw Abe a half dollar. This was the most money Abe had ever earned in one day.

What would you do for fun?

Contests were a lot of fun.

There were weight-lifting contests and wrestling contests. There were jumping and running contests. There were contests to see who was the strongest, or who could throw the farthest, or who was the fastest runner. Abe almost always won first place in these contests.

Boys and girls made their own toys. They made jump ropes from grapevines in the

woods. They made their own balls. They wrapped yarn around a little stone. Then they covered it with buckskin.

They played some of the games you play today. They played hide-and-seek, prisoner's base, and hare and hounds. They sang and played "Skip to My Lou."

But there was so much work to do on the frontier that there was not much time just for fun. So people managed to have fun when they were working.

People often worked together. If a new cabin had to be built, men and boys got together for a house raising.

With so many people helping, it didn't take long to put up a cabin.

While the men and boys were working, the women and girls were busy cooking. When the cabin was finished, it was time for everybody to eat and have fun.

Women and girls got together for sewing and quilting bees. They talked as they sewed clothes and made quilts, and the work seemed to go faster.

You could even have fun husking a pile of corn. At a cornhusking bee, boys formed into two teams. Boys on each team worked fast to pull off the husks from the ears of corn. The team that finished first won.

If a boy found a red ear of corn among the yellow ones, he could kiss any girl he chose.

Would you go to school?

Most of the time you wouldn't go to school.

Schools on the frontier were open only two or three months of the year. Usually school was open in the winter when children were not needed to help with the farmwork.

If the teacher moved away, school would close. If another teacher came along, the school would open again for a while.

Many people never did learn to read or write.

Abe Lincoln began going to school when he was six years old. He went to school whenever he had the chance.

But all his days of schooling added together did not come to one whole year.

What kind of school would you go to?

You would go to a *blab school*! The schools were called blab schools because everyone blabbed — that is, everyone said his lessons out loud at the same time. That is how the teacher could tell if each pupil was doing his work.

Boys and girls of all ages learned together in one room. Six-year-olds were in the same class with sixteen-year-olds.

The pupils were called scholars. The teacher was called a schoolmaster.

Blab schools were not free. Parents had to pay the schoolmaster a dollar or two for each scholar. Some schoolmasters took their pay in deerskins or vegetables.

What did the schoolhouse look like?

The schoolhouse on the frontier was just another log cabin.

You would sit on a hard bench made of a log split in half. The benches had no backs.

Many schoolhouses had no windows and only a dirt floor. A fire in the fireplace kept the room warm. If you sat too near the fire, you would be too hot. If you sat too far away, you would be too cold.

You might live miles away from a schoolhouse. When he lived in Indiana, Abe Lincoln had to walk about four miles through the woods to get to school.

What were the teachers like?

Schoolmasters were strict!

If you didn't know your lessons, the school-master would call you a dunce. He would make you wear a long pointed duncecap on your head. You would have to stand in the corner with your face to the wall.

Schoolmasters kept a bundle of switches handy. If you didn't behave, you would feel the sharp whack of the schoolmaster's switch. Or he might make you hold out your hand. Then he would smack it with a ruler.

Some schoolmasters traveled from one settlement to another.

Some schoolmasters were farmers who taught school for a few months in the wintertime.

Some schoolmasters did not know much more than the boys and girls they taught. It was not long before Abe Lincoln knew more than many schoolmasters.

What would you learn in school?

You would learn how to read and how to do simple arithmetic.

The scholars took turns reading the Bible.

Spelling was important, too. No one cared if you knew the meaning of the word or not. The most important thing was to spell it right. You would study spelling in a book called

Dilworth's Speller. You could learn many things besides spelling in *Dilworth's Speller*. You could learn how to count, and how to speak and write correctly. You could learn the names of states and their capitals.

One of Abe Lincoln's schoolmasters taught good manners. He taught the children the right way to greet a stranger. He made the girls stand up and curtsey. He made the boys stand up and bow.

If you went to school with Abe, you would say he was the best scholar in school. He was good at arithmetic. He could read better than anyone else, and he came in first in spelling contests.

If you wanted to be the best scholar, you would have to study as hard as Abe did.

*How would you practice writing
and arithmetic?*

Paper cost too much to use for practice. If you wanted to practice writing, you would do the same thing Abe Lincoln did. He wrote with a stick in the dirt. And he wrote on a wooden shovel with a burnt stick. When the shovel was covered with letters, Abe scraped them off and began writing again.

Abe's handwriting was so good that the neighbors asked him to write their letters for them.

You would use your notebook to copy down arithmetic rules you wanted to remember. The notebook was called a copybook.

When you wrote in your copybook, you used a goose feather or a feather from a wild turkey for a pen. This was called a quill pen. You wrote with ink made from the root of a blackberry bush and a special kind of iron called copperas.

What books did children read?

People on the frontier did not often buy storybooks for children. And most children did not read much anyhow.

But Abe Lincoln read everything he could. He used to say, "The things I want to know are in books. My best friend is a man who will get me a book I ain't read."

If you were Abe's friend, he would tell you stories from the books he read.

These are some of the books Abe read:

The Bible. The Bible was often the only book people on the frontier owned. When Abe and his sister Sarah learned to read, they took turns reading the Bible out loud on Sundays.

Aesop's Fables. Abe loved these stories about animals that talked and acted like people.

Robinson Crusoe. Abe's stepmother gave this book to Abe. It was about a man who was shipwrecked and who lived on an island.

The Arabian Nights. This book was full of
stories of magic and make-believe. One of
Abe's favorite stories in the book was the story
of "Sinbad the Sailor." Abe liked to tell how
Sinbad sailed his boat near a rock. The rock
acted like a magnet. It pulled all the nails out
of the boat. The boat fell apart, and Sinbad
fell into the water.

Abe would walk miles to borrow a book.
He borrowed books about Benjamin Franklin
and George Washington. George Washington
became his hero.

What were the biggest dangers on the frontier?

Wolves. If you camped out in the woods at night, you would have to keep a fire going to keep the wolves away.

Weather. Sometimes there were heavy rains that flooded the land and spoiled the crops. Sometimes there was not enough rain to grow crops. And sometimes there were heavy snows that killed many of the animals.

Sickness. Sickness was the biggest danger of all.

There were not many doctors. When Abe

Lincoln was growing up in Indiana, the nearest doctor was thirty-five miles away from his cabin.

There were no drugstores. People made their own medicines from plants called herbs.

How would you travel?

Traveling on the frontier was hard.

The roads were bad. In many places there were no roads at all. People had to chop down trees to make a road through the woods.

There were no trains in the wilderness. Railroad trains did not begin to run in the United States until Abe Lincoln was twenty-one years old. And they did not run as far west as Indiana.

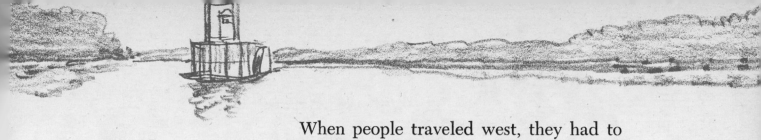

When people traveled west, they had to walk or go on horseback or ride in wagons or in stagecoaches pulled by horses. Or they could go part way by water.

Traveling west by land was hard.

It was much easier to travel by water. People floated down the rivers in canoes and big flatboats. Or they went on the handsome new steamboats.

When Abe was nineteen, he and a friend took some cargo to New Orleans. They rode down the Mississippi River on a flatboat. The trip was more than a thousand miles. It took them many weeks to get to New Orleans. Abe and his friend went back by steamboat. It took them only a week to get home.

What was New Salem like?

The village of New Salem, Illinois, was new and growing when Abe Lincoln came to town in the year 1831. He was twenty-two years old.

There was a mill in New Salem. There were a few stores, and there were about twelve families who lived in log cabins.

Farmers came from fifty miles away. They brought their wheat to the mill to be turned into flour. They might stop at a store to buy salt or a new tool or a pretty bonnet.

More and more people came to live in New Salem, and the town grew. Soon there were twenty-five log cabins and about a hundred people.

It was the largest town Abe had ever lived in. He stayed there for six years.

Who lived and worked in New Salem?

If you lived in New Salem, you would know everybody in town. Abe did.

Joshua Miller was the blacksmith. He made iron shoes for horses and for oxen. He made iron nails, pots, and tools. If you needed a wagon, you might ask Mr. Miller to make one for you. The blacksmith of New Salem could also make wagons.

Or you might ask Robert Johnson to make you a wagon. He was a busy man. He was the cabinetmaker and the wheelwright. As a cabinetmaker, he made furniture. As a wheelwright, he made wagons, carts, and spinning wheels.

If you wanted a new hat, you would go to Martin Waddell, the town hatter.

If you needed a pair of leather shoes, you would go first to Philemon Morris, the tanner. He made leather from animal skins.

Then you would take the leather to the cobbler, Peter Lukins. Mr. Lukins made new shoes and mended old ones.

There were two doctors, a minister, and an innkeeper in town. There was a schoolmaster, Mentor Graham, who helped Abe learn how to speak and write correctly.

50

Old Granny Spears would tell you about the time she was stolen by the Indians when she was a young girl.

Jack Kelso would go fishing with you and recite poetry by the hour. Abe listened, and he began to love poetry.

What was a store in New Salem like?

Abe Lincoln worked in a store at New Salem.

All the people in town knew they could trust Abe. One day a woman came into the store to buy some cloth. After she left, Abe found out that she had paid him six cents too much. That night Abe walked six miles to her house to give the woman back her money.

Later, Abe and William Berry became partners and opened a store of their own.

You could buy all sorts of things at their store. Some of the things they sold came from the eastern states.

They sold seeds and saddles, needles and thread, cloth and dishes, guns and tools, and tallow for making candles.

They sold cheese and bacon, butter and eggs, coffee, tea, and whiskey.

Abe Lincoln's store was a good place for friends to get together. They liked to hear Abe tell stories and jokes.

When Abe wasn't busy at the store, he read books. At night he slept on the store counter.

What happened when you got sick in New Salem?

If you were very sick, you might call Dr. Allen to take care of you.

But most of the time people took medicines they made themselves. They made medicines from herbs, roots, bark of trees, and even tobacco juice. They made a medicine out of tiny bits of pewter, which they scraped from pewter spoons.

People said whiskey was a good cure for a stomach ache.

To cure a cold or a sore throat, they said, take a piece of meat with pepper on it and wrap it around the sick person's throat.

Some people had strange ideas about what caused sickness. They said that if a horse breathed on a child, the child would get whooping cough.

People had strange ideas about how to cure warts, too. Steal a dishrag and hide it in a tree, they said, and the wart will go away.

If a snake bit you, you might go to Uncle Jimmy Pantier. People said he could cure snake bites by rubbing the bite and saying some words no one could understand.

Some people said that Uncle Johnny Watkins had a better cure. He would put a flat stone over the snake bite. Next, he would drop the stone into sweetened milk and put it over the snake bite again. Some people said Uncle Johnny's stone was a sure cure.

How would you send a letter?

If you wanted to send a letter, you would give it to the postmaster. Abe Lincoln was postmaster of New Salem for three years.

You would write your letter on a sheet of paper.

There were no envelopes. So you would fold the paper and seal the folds with hot sealing wax. You wrote the address on the outside.

There were no stamps either. In the upper right-hand corner, the postmaster wrote down how much it would cost to send the letter. But you wouldn't pay to send the letter. The person who got the letter paid for it. The farther away he lived, the more he had to pay.

If you wrote a letter on one sheet of paper to a friend who lived thirty miles away, your friend would have to pay six cents. But if you used two sheets of paper, your friend would have to pay twice as much. So people tried to crowd everything onto one sheet of paper.

The stagecoach came through town every week. Letters and newspapers for the people of New Salem were dropped off at the post office. Letters to be mailed were picked up.

If people did not come for their mail, Abe would take it to them. Sometimes he walked many miles to deliver a letter that he thought was important. He put the letters in his hat. People said Abe Lincoln carried the post office around in his hat.

What was Springfield like?

Springfield, Illinois, was a much bigger town than New Salem.

Abraham Lincoln came to Springfield in 1837 to be a lawyer. He was twenty-eight years old.

Lincoln lived in Springfield for twenty-four years. He saw the town grow to be an important city with ten thousand people.

When Lincoln came to town, there were about a thousand people living there.

The center of the town was the public square. Around the square were the court-house, the jail, and some stores.

Springfield had six grocery stores, four drugstores, and a bookstore. Women could do their fashion buying at nineteen dry-goods stores. They could buy such things as cloth, ribbons, buttons, gloves, laces, and thread.

Springfield had six churches, two schools, and four hotels.

There were hatters and tailors, shoemakers and watchmakers, painters and carpenters, blacksmiths and wagonmakers, and a barber. There were eleven lawyers and eighteen doctors.

At night, the city was dark. There were no lamps to light the streets.

There were no sidewalks in town. In the summer, the streets were dusty. In the winter, they were muddy. Cows, chickens, and hogs walked around everywhere.

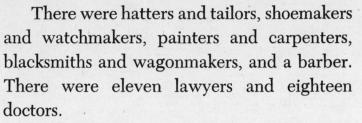

What kind of houses would you
see in Springfield?

If you moved to Springfield when Lincoln did, you would see a few log cabins. You would see some fine big houses, too.

But most of the people lived in small wooden houses. Other wooden buildings were in the back of the house: a woodshed, a toilet called a privy, a carriage house where people kept their buggy or wagon, and a barn for the family's horse and cow.

Abraham Lincoln got married in 1842 when he was thirty-three years old. Two years later he and his wife Mary, and their baby son, moved into a house of their own.

At first Mary Lincoln did all the housework herself. She cooked, cleaned the house, sewed clothes, and made soap and candles.

Lincoln helped too. He kept the woodbox filled. He milked the cow and took care of the horse.

What did people in Springfield do for fun?

The people of Springfield loved parties and fancy balls.

In 1857, Mary Lincoln wrote to her sister: "Within the last three weeks, there has been a party almost every night."

People went to the theater to see plays. They went to concerts to hear music and songs. They went to lectures to hear famous men talk.

Lincoln went to the theater and to concerts and to fancy balls. But the best times were the hours he spent playing with his sons. He loved to spin tops and play marbles with them.

The circus came to Springfield twice a year. There were parades, bands, animals, and clowns.

The star of one circus was a Learned Pig who could tell time and play cards with the people in the audience.

Holidays were always fun. On Christmas, children set off firecrackers. New Year's Day was a day for visiting and for eating oysters, ice cream, cake, and candy. There were picnics and parades on the Fourth of July. There were firecrackers, of course, and band music, and long speeches.

But the best day of all was the day Abraham Lincoln was nominated for President of the United States. A hundred guns were fired. In the public square, people shouted for joy. All the bells in town rang. Flags waved. A brass band played in front of Lincoln's house. A great crowd shouted for a speech.

Lincoln told the crowd he wished his house was big enough so that he could ask them all to come inside.

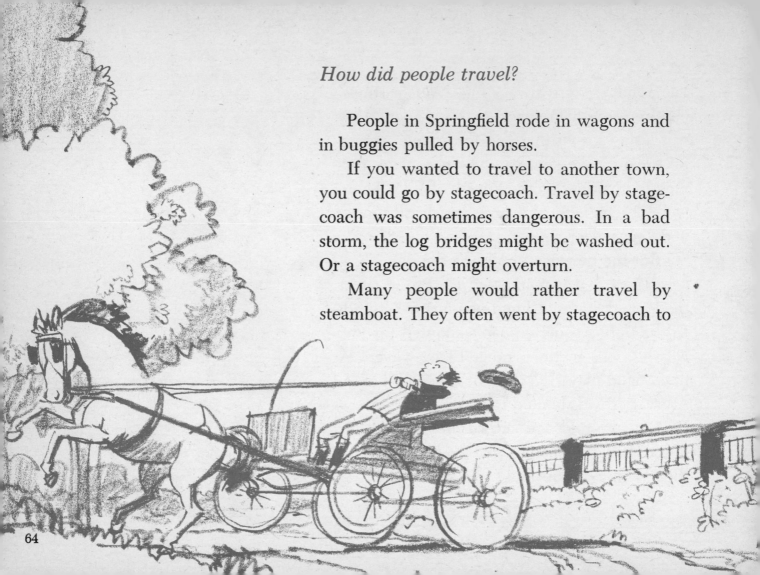

How did people travel?

People in Springfield rode in wagons and in buggies pulled by horses.

If you wanted to travel to another town, you could go by stagecoach. Travel by stage-coach was sometimes dangerous. In a bad storm, the log bridges might be washed out. Or a stagecoach might overturn.

Many people would rather travel by steamboat. They often went by stagecoach to a river, where they would continue their trip on a steamboat.

In 1842, five years after Lincoln moved to Springfield, the first train came into town.

Trains had been running in the East for about twelve years. Now many miles of railroad tracks were being laid farther west.

People called the train the "Iron Horse" or "The Dragon That Breathed Sparks."

They said trains traveled "almost as fast as birds fly — fifteen or twenty miles an hour."

Every year, more and more people went places by train.

When Lincoln was elected to the United States Congress, he took his family to Washington with him. They traveled part of the way by stagecoach and part of the way by train.

What kind of clothes did people wear in Springfield?

When Lincoln was a boy in Indiana, he wore deerskin moccasins. In Springfield he wore leather shoes.

Everybody wore shoes. Now when farmers' wives came to town, they were no longer barefoot.

When farmers came to town, they wore pantaloons made in the cloth mills of Massachusetts. They did not have to kill deer and tan the hides to make buckskin breeches.

When Lincoln was a boy, he wore a coonskin cap. In Springfield he wore a tall black hat made of silk or of beaver fur. It was called a stovepipe or a plug hat.

When Lincoln was postmaster of New Salem, he carried letters in his hat. And when he was a lawyer in Springfield he carried papers in his hat. Into his hat went newspaper clippings and notes he wanted to remember.

Women in Springfield read *Godey's Lady's Book* to see the latest dresses from New York and from Paris, France. They copied the

patterns to make their own dresses. They made long dresses with wide sleeves and tiny waists.

There were many parties in Springfield. Women could buy velvet, silk, and satin cloth to make ball gowns. They could buy lace veils, handkerchiefs, silk fans, and flowered bonnets.

What could you buy in Springfield?

If you lived in Springfield just before Lincoln was elected President, you could buy many things that used to be made at home.

When Lincoln was a boy, all the clothes were made by hand. Women spent hours working at their spinning wheels and looms.

But machines changed that. Machines were invented that used water power and steam power to make them go.

Machines spun thread and wove it into cloth. Hundreds of people had jobs running machines in the factories and mills of New England.

Cloth and other things made in factories were sent from New England to stores all over the United States.

Cotton cloth cost about three cents a yard. Women in Springfield bought cotton, wool, and silk cloth.

They bought sheets, towels, curtains, and tablecloths that were made on the new sewing machines.

Stores in Springfield sold factory-made gloves, hats, and shoes. You could buy steel pens, buttons, clocks, carpets, and silverplated knives and forks and spoons.

People no longer spent days making their own soap and candles. Soap and candles were sold in the stores for a few cents.

When Lincoln was a boy, he had never heard of rubber balls and balloons. Now he could buy these toys for his sons.

More and more farmers were buying new machines to make their work easier. One man running a machine could do as much work as ten men.

There was a machine to shell corn. The farmer turned a crank to make the machine work. A machine called a reaper cut wheat. Horses pulled the reaper across the field.

A farmer could take his vegetables to market in a wagon with iron springs.

A farmer's wife did not have to cook over the fireplace. She could use her new iron stove. And she could keep foods fresh in an icebox.

What were the changes you would see in Springfield?

If you lived in Springfield as long as Lincoln did, you would see many changes. Lincoln lived in Springfield for twenty-four years.

When the Lincolns first moved into their house, they could look out of their kitchen window and see corn growing. Soon the Lincolns could see only houses where the corn once grew.

Springfield soon became the capital city of Illinois.

The few log cabins that were left were torn down. In their place stood fine houses made of wood or brick. More and more stores and hotels were built around the public square.

In 1853, a visiting newspaperman wrote: "Just think of a city without a single good side-walk in it, or even a public lamp to light a street."

That year lampposts were built and gas lamps lit up the square.

Seven years later the city put in sidewalks around the square. They were made of wooden planks.

When Lincoln first moved to Springfield in 1837, there was only one policeman. There were no fire engines. Twenty years later, in 1857, Springfield got its first fire engine. And by the time Lincoln was elected President, in 1860, there were five policemen.

With the invention of the telegraph, news came to Springfield faster than ever. It was in the telegraph office of Springfield that Lincoln got the news that he was elected President.

*Some important changes that happened
during Lincoln's lifetime.*

If you grew up with Abraham Lincoln, you would
see great changes from the time Lincoln was a
boy in Kentucky and Indiana to the time he was
President in Washington, D.C.

Important changes took place in transportation. When Lincoln was a boy, there were no trains at all.

It took a long time to send a message by stagecoach. By the time Lincoln was a grown man, the telegraph was invented. Messages could be sent very quickly.

Lincoln's mother cooked over a fireplace. When Lincoln was a lawyer in Springfield, his wife cooked on a stove like this.

Women on the frontier made their own cloth. Later, more and more women could buy cloth made in factories.

When Lincoln was a boy, men did not have machines to help them farm. By the time Lincoln became President, many farmers were using machines like this.

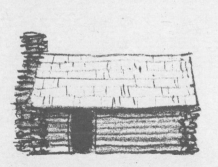 

When Lincoln lived in a log cabin on the frontier, he never dreamed that one day he would live in this house.